Cancer-Us

It was me. Is it you?

DYWUANA SYKES

Cancer-Us

It was me. Is it you?

Detect and Treat the Inner Agents That are Destroying
You

DYWUANA SYKES

DEDICATION

This book is dedicated to the memory of all my loved ones who sought treatment yet in the end did not survive the dreaded effects of their cancer conditions. It is further dedicated to every survivor of every cancer who views each day as a gift from God with intentional purpose to maximize every remaining moment.

CONTENTS

FOREWORD

Bold! Fresh! Rich! No, I'm not describing a food item but the first book by Dywuana Sykes, which proved to be "Food for the Soul."

Bold! As a cancer survivor, Mrs. Sykes passionately speaks from first-hand experience of the devastating effects cancer can have on a person's physical, emotional, spiritual and even social being.

Fresh! Statistics state that 1 out of 3 will experience cancer. But according to Mrs. Sykes, 3 out of 3 will experience cancer. Whether it is unhealthy relationships or difficult work environment or even a church dispute, cancer will spring up in individuals. And this cancer is not from outside but from within.

Rich! Packed with practical how-to's, spiritual insight and inspirational truths, Mrs. Sykes reveals how everyone can "live in the present" and become healthy as they navigate the future God has for them.

Whatever your "cancer" diagnosis may be, reading this book will leave you believing and ready for your next journey.

Bartholomew Orr

ACKNOWLEDGMENTS

In looking back over my life, specifically, my journey through cancer, there are so many I would like to offer my gratitude.

I must give a big shout out to Wealthy Sisters Network founder, Dawniel Winningham for the push to focus on survivorship utilizing my passion for helping others to live their dreams and for the referral to Je Tuan Lavyonne.

Thank you Je Tuan for your literary expertise and friendship. You pushed me to reveal more about my life and cancer journey than I ever would have otherwise. You were so instrumental in helping me bring my words, my story, to life. I'm so thankful for the amount of time you spent with me.

I thank God for divinely positioning me with Dr. Michael Berry-my breast surgeon, Dr. Jarvis Reed-my oncologist, my primary nurse Cynthia Rose and the entire staff at the West Clinic who were so instrumental in my treatment and healing. A very special thanks to my chemotherapy nurse, Avis Williams, who treated me with the highest care and eased my concerns by answering all of my questions about the medicines I received.

I thank God for my friends, coworkers and confidantes, Jada Jackson and Michelle Martin, who were my "ride or die" mates. You attended the doctor's appointments with me and my mom. You took notes so my mom and I could just soak in what was happening. You were a tremendous support and I will forever be grateful for your kindness to me. And of course, Effie Landers, who took the load off of my family by agreeing to transport me to each and every chemotherapy treatment except one! Wow, what a sacrifice you made for me. I can't forget Janice Triplett, my prayer partner and friend, who sacrificed the comforts of her own home, to ensure that every night immediately following treatment I was not alone as my husband continued to travel and make a living for us. To all of my former bosses and coworkers who supported me-Thank You!!!

To my pastor, Dr. Bartholomew Orr and his lovely wife, Valarie! The love and support you personally gave to me will always be remembered. You are the most humble leaders who operate a big congregation with the mindset and feelings of a small family church. Your vision and leadership enabled me to experience God through Brown Baptist Sunday Service in the comforts of my home as I recuperated for the months I intentionally stayed away while taking chemotherapy. Thank you for your love and support.

To my parents, you have always been there for me. You have tirelessly supported the fulfillment of all my dreams. You always step in to assist with my little angel and you made sure that as I spent countless hours working on this project and travelling, my family and home were cared for. So much of what I do and what drives me has everything to do with you.

To my husband, I know my dreams often overwhelm you but it's as if God gives you peace to trust my choices. Thank you for your support and encouragement and push to continue when I've wanted to turn back to the familiar as I trek ahead on unchartered territory. Your faith in me and the things God has placed in me will forever be remembered. Thank you.

To my heavenly Father, for a relationship in which you have shown me patience, forgiveness and unmatched love. Thank you God for all of the wilderness experiences you have allowed in my life which have served to draw me closer to you. Thank you for all of the divine, miraculous and supernatural ways you have spoken to me, including the insight you have given me for this book.

Isaiah 26: 3-4 *"Thou wilt keep him in perfect peace, whose mind is stayed on thee: because he trusteth in thee. Trust ye in the Lord for ever: for in the Lord Jehovah is everlasting strength:"*

{1}

THE TRUTH ABOUT CANCER

Cancer, a disease many fear as life ending, has been totally life transforming for me. I want to start out with a clear definition of what cancer is. According to Cancer.gov:

"Cancer is a term used for diseases in which abnormal cells divide without control and are able to invade other tissues (of the body). Cancer cells can spread to other parts (not initially affected) of the body through the blood and lymph systems."

This definition became extremely important to me and even changed my life. I hope that it will change yours too.

Not On My Christmas Wish List

Christmas is ideally a joyous occasion for families, and ours is no exception. During the Christmas week of 2010, my mother and I were anticipating our immediate family finally being under the same roof for the celebration. My oldest brother had just retired from the Air Force and my mother was ecstatic about a gathering at her house for the holiday.

I can still remember getting the diagnosis on that Monday, just a few days before we would celebrate our most favorite time of the year. "Mrs. Sykes, I'm sorry to have to tell you but it does appear you have cancer." I did not know how my mother would react to the news, so two of my closest friends went with me for support. When I broke the news she said, "I knew something was going to happen to put a damper on our Christmas celebration this year." I assured my mother that she did not have any reason to be worried or concerned about the Christmas festivities going off without a hitch.

That day I made the decision my cancer journey was not going to be that kind of experience. I know you are probably thinking my mother's response and focus on anything other than me was absurd. After all, I had just found out I had cancer. Did I not deserve to have all of the focus on me? While it may be true I deserved some special attention, it was not what I wanted at that moment. I am confident of my mother's love for me and what became clear right away was this would not be my journey to travel alone. When a person travels the path of cancer diagnosis, the people who love them go through it too.

I chose the positive thoughts and reactions I wanted to have and this had a direct impact on how my family and friends walked through this journey with me. My mother recalls how she began to cry at the first mention of my diagnosis. However, as she saw me standing there exhibiting such strength in the moment, she told herself to dry those tears and be the strength she saw in me. I am sure my mother and I could have created a pool of tears in that moment, but already our thoughts were of victory. From the very beginning, I decided I was a conqueror.

Yes, I had many trials, some of which I will highlight throughout this book. I am just convinced some decisions must be made at the very beginning of your trial. One of the most important I believe is this- Is the situation going to overtake you? On the other hand, are you going to overcome it? In my opinion, the real battle takes place in your mind.

I have always said my situation was a win-win. I accepted Jesus as Lord and Savior of my life at a young age. Although I have not always acted in ways that reflected that choice, I was confident of the hope I confessed in Christ. I knew where I placed my faith and I knew that God was in complete control.

I asked God to help me go out gracefully if this was my intended exit. I did pray, however, that He would allow me to stick around a little longer for my daughter, who was only two years old when I was diagnosed with cancer. I just wanted the opportunity to pour into her all of the things of God I had received and to share my life experiences both good and bad in hopes that they would be life lessons for her as well. Beyond that one request, I was good with my outcome and His purpose for allowing this season in my life.

I am totally convinced I went through my cancer journey for reasons much greater than just being able to boast of being a survivor. God has given me an assignment to expand our thinking about the cancers that exist in our lives. I am here to let others know that whatever the diagnosis, there can be victories along the difficult journey.

For the record, the Christmas celebration was wonderful. I shared the news of my diagnosis with my immediate family, and we all still enjoyed the greatest "birth" day of the year. Looking back, I believe this was the beginning of many "births" to come. Cancer was not an immediate death sentence and I refused to live what time I had in a state of doom and gloom.

My Initial View of Cancer

Prior to my diagnosis, I thought that cancer was a foreign substance that found a way to invade the body. I thought that outside sources or chemicals came in and caused contamination to the body. Then there was the big revelation! When I found out that it was your body's own cells functioning abnormally, dividing without control and destroying the tissues of the body, I was shocked. Getting clear about what was really happening inside of my body was eye-opening for me.

How It All Began

I went for my annual mammogram which typically was brief but that was not the case this time around. I got a call back and the radiologist told me there was an area of concern that she would like to re-test. I was assured this was very common. She asked me if I could come the next day. I was pretty consumed with my job as we were in the middle of a busy period and I asked her if I could put my retest off until the next week because that timeframe would be better for me. She said, "Oh sure." I was really laidback about this process, until I actually returned to the clinic and began a very different examination process.

When I arrived at the return appointment, I noticed that the radiologist spent a lot more time with me than she normally did on my routine mammogram screenings. After we finished the initial imaging, she had me return to the waiting room. She wanted to confer with the doctor to see if any additional images would be needed. At that moment, I realized this was serious.

I did have to go back one more time for one more round of images, and then they had me go and meet with a counselor. At this time, they did not say I had breast cancer, but they did tell me I had to have a biopsy. They gave me this little card with a poem. It was interesting, and it read:

A Prayer of Strength

Do not look forward to the changes and

Chances of this life in fear rather look to them

With full hope that, as they arise, God will

Deliver you out of them.

He has kept you hitherto, do you but hold fast

To His dear hand, and He will lead you safely

Through all things; and, when you cannot

Stand, He will bear you in His arms.

Do not look forward to what may happen

Tomorrow; the same everlasting Father who

Cares for you today will take care of you

Tomorrow and everyday

Either He will shield you from suffering, or

He will give you unfailing strength to bear it.

Be at peace then and put aside all anxious

Thoughts and imaginations!

I left the clinic with a height of emotions and got in my car. I will be honest; this is probably one of the few times within this journey I completely broke down. I did not want to call my mom because I knew it would tear her up to hear me having a meltdown. Therefore, I called my oldest brother, and I just told him "I know." At that moment, I knew I had cancer. I did not need a biopsy to confirm this for me. The way they presented the information to me gave me an indication they were already sure about my diagnosis.

From a spiritual perspective, I was thinking about my life and everything I had experienced. I knew that God was not going to let me off the hook in this instance with a "negative" diagnosis. Considering He had delivered me from the hands of a crack addicted gunman more than 19 years earlier, I knew this story was going to be bigger. He was preparing me for my next journey not by causing but rather allowing this moment. Through what seemed to be a never ending flow of tears, I explained to my brother the process of my return visit and my feelings about my condition. He refused to join me in that place, but rather, he kept a positive outlook and became the strength I needed for that moment.

He said, "We're not going to believe anything until we get a final report. We're going to keep believing in faith." Then he prayed over me. I began to recall a family get-together just a month prior where several family members were dealing with pains, including my nephew who had suffered a minor injury in his college football game. Before we departed, I felt led to pray for them. I remember saying "I pray for all things spoken and not spoken." Little did I know I would have the greatest hurdle to cross-CANCER!

After that conversation with my brother, I vowed to stay present with every aspect of the process.

Things May get Worse before they get Better

I did have a biopsy and the doctors told me nine times out of ten, scenarios like mine have benign results. They said the odds were in my favor. I am telling you this because even when you are disappointed, even when things look like they should go your way and they do not, you still can get through them. I had free will to choose to be mad and bitter at God. However, I knew there was a greater purpose.

My initial diagnosis was stage 0. I had never even heard of it.

However, it meant I had a small area that was "noninvasive," somewhat contained and not affecting tissues yet. While mastectomy was an option, the treatment plan I chose was lumpectomy, radiation, and Tamoxifen, a 5 year pill that would essentially retrain my cells not to think or act as cancer cells. The goal of the lumpectomy would be to clear a certain amount of margin around the affected area, which would be confirmed microscopically once removed.

There was good news and bad news right after the surgery. Good news, the margins were adequately cleared with my lumpectomy. Bad news, the review under the microscope found that the cancer was invasive (had broken through and potentially affected other tissues). I needed another surgery to check my lymph nodes. The second surgery did reveal a tumor in my second lymph node, and that is a pretty big deal. Many people think once cancer cells get into the lymph nodes, you are toast and this is not true.

What started out as a simple surgery requiring only two weeks of sick leave from work ended up resulting in five months out of the office and many noticeable changes for me. It was such a downer for my co-workers. They went on the journey with me too. It was disheartening to keep sending them updated news that appeared as if my diagnosis was getting worse and worse with each report, especially when the original treatment plan seemed so simple. I found myself sending them inspiration and telling them to stay encouraged.

They would continuously inquire about my condition and my boss at the time did her best to reassure them everything would be okay. I remember taking the reins and sending a direct note myself telling them to be encouraged--that I would be back with them as soon as I could. I encouraged them to continue to check-in and I would respond when I could. I told them in a letter "If I'm slow to respond, just know it's an uphill journey and I'm still climbing. It may get a little tough but I'm climbing nonetheless." Just thinking about this still chokes me up a bit. I still felt the urge to inspire others while I was going through my own struggle.

All of this leads to my next point. Be careful not to get offended when people feel bad for you and your condition. Those that love you will have a hard time seeing you go through the ills and pains of cancer so do not invalidate their feelings. Everyone has his or her own definition of what cancer means and unfortunately most of the world considers it an immediate death sentence. Be careful not to allow anyone else to inflict his or her fears upon you. You are a survivor, not a victim! There will always be lots of attention on you as a survivor. Allow the attention to be a source of inspiration for others.

Stay Present and in the Moment

As you can see, situations can change and sometimes get worse before they get better. Immediately after my surgeon called to reveal the "good news, bad news," my mother ranted, "Do the doctors even know what they're doing? When are they going to get it together?"
I said, "Momma, listen. Every day they find something else is a plus for us. They're finding it and they're fixing it."

I did not try to reject any of the information. I did not fight against it, and I did not say, 'Whoa, why is this happening to me?' I stayed present with it. I accepted my situation. I spent time reading the research on my diagnosis. Of course it became clear my condition was a bit worse than what was thought just days earlier but I had confidence we were working towards a solution. My thoughts were, "We've got a diagnosis, and we've got prescribed treatments, so let's roll with it."

I did not spend a lot of time getting multiple opinions. I have seen people die in situations because they are so busy fighting their truth. I understand everyone has his or her own belief systems. I am not saying chemotherapy is the only option for treatment, or that one doctor's opinion has to be your law. I just want it to be clear that there is a distinct difference between faith and denial. There are some trials and conditions through which we must trek. The reality of life is that God will not remove every cup from us.

Your course of treatment is your choice. I have heard an old saying "pick your horse and ride it". You can definitely get a second opinion, but eventually you have to get to a place of surrender. You do not have to surrender to the cancer, but you do have to surrender to the process. When I stayed present and surrendered to what was actually happening God was able to do what He does best. When I surrendered to what God was doing in my life, He was able to use it for His glory.

I know things often seem easier said than done, and sure, there are many struggles that come with cancer. Oftentimes people will place permanent labels on you such as being "sick" or "having cancer". I have walked through this experience in a very inspiring way. My prayer is that through this book you will be better equipped to:

- Early detect the cancerous conditions in your life

- Determine what the treatment plan should be to ensure you are healed

- Garner the appropriate support system to aid in your healing

- Better manage the side effects by understanding on the onset what they are

- Embrace the blessings of surviving

- Transform your thoughts about your past

- Get clear on your God-given purpose

- Release the fears that limit you and

- Walk through your life's journey, with all that unfolds, victoriously.

Throughout my life, I often envision Satan, our adversary, having a conversation with God about me much like he did concerning Job. This time, God asked Satan if he'd considered me. God decided He could trust me with a little trouble. Today, I am still honored.

{2}

DO YOU HAVE IT?

My life forever changed when I realized what cancer was. My own cells-acting abnormally, rapidly dividing out of control and destroying the tissues of my body. Cells, the smallest structural unit of an organism capable of independent functioning. (Yahoo dictionary). I thought about how churches form "cell" groups when their membership reaches a certain size in an attempt to keep each member connected to a more functional size group. When I understood that tissues of the body are cells and other matter acting together to perform specific functions in the body, I realized we all have the potential for cancer-not just in the physical body but in every facet of our lives.

With every opportunity we have to function within a collective unit, there lies the potential for agents to act abnormal, cause division and destroy the very essence of the group to which they are purposefully connected. These groups include but are not limited to family, church, work, personal relationships, as well as political, civil and social groups. There are many untreated cancers of this type that exist. These unspoken cancers are becoming epidemics, often producing damaging and even deadly outcomes when allowed to go untreated.

While preparing to speak about my breast cancer journey for the very first time in 2011, God spoke to me and said, "You've had cancer before." He was absolutely right! I had not been limited to breast cancer. I realized I had allowed abnormal activity to exist for years in my relationships with men and I allowed my heart to be hardened by my experiences in the workplace. These were two areas of my life that required aggressive treatment because they were destroying my self-esteem, my passion, my life!

Abnormalities in my Relationships

I continuously made unhealthy choices when it came to relationships with men. I would find myself in one toxic relationship after the next. I entered every relationship with the mindset that he was "the one" without even an evaluation of what he realistically had to offer me. If he found interest in me, that was enough and I cast all my time and energy there.

I had a cancerous condition that continued to exist for more than 18 years of my life. I felt like I could help others change and in contrast found myself always operating in a state of codependency. I thought the light in me was enough to help clean up the darkness in the men I allowed in my life, and it was not. The time and energy I spent trying to "fix" the men in my relationships generated me nothing but heartache. These relationships ate away my self-esteem.

I want to be clear that I was actively involved in church, doing all the right things, singing and serving-yet slowly dying on the inside. One day in a fit of despair after yet another failed relationship, I asked the Lord, "Help me to find the love in you, I continue to seek in men." I wish I could tell you I had immediate deliverance from this condition but it was several years later before true deliverance came.

The big blow occurred three years later in my life when again I made the choice to get involved with someone I knew was not right for me. Looking back, perhaps I thought it was my only hope – after all, many of my friends had married and were beginning to have families. This choice however would prove to be my greatest mistake of all. I had yoked up with a crack addict and any thought I had of leaving him would be met with violent opposition. In the end, I had to flee the state and return home to live with my parents with only my purse and the clothes I had on my back.

I was an educated woman with a Master's degree, just having recently passed the Certified Public Accountants Exam, yet I continued to fail in relationships. It hurt that I could not seem to get it right. I remember feeling so depressed and like such a failure. There were days I did not have the strength to get out of the bed on my own. My dad would force me out and every morning we would walk. Sometimes I would cry for the entire walk. My dad would encourage me and say, "Keep walking." That had become my mantra. I had to keep walking through the pain of failure and bad choices. Little did I realize walking was a part of my treatment and healing in this cancer and the physical cancer, which was to come.

I stayed with my parents for a short while. My job search initially resulted in several dead ends. I was growing impatient and I felt hopeless. One evening, in a moment of frustration, I decided I was going back to the relationship I fled – yes the crack-addict I left running away from- with only the clothes on my back and my purse. I decided I was going to leave my parents a note and tell them how much I appreciated everything they had done for me. I planned to tell them not to come looking for me anymore.

In that moment, going back to my past hurt felt better than moving forward into something new with the current struggles of such an unknown future. I was confident the job market would be better in the city I had fled and I was open to going back to the person I knew was dangerous for me. I even called him to tell him I was coming back. Would you believe he rejected me? That was my rock bottom. I paced the hallway, I was having a full on panic attack. My thoughts were not clear. I called my mom who was away visiting a sick relative, but she was unable to answer her phone. My dad was in the house, but he was sound asleep and unaware of the turmoil I was in. I went to the bathroom and I got down on my knees. I did not say a lot to God, but what I did say came from the deepest place inside of me. I groaned deeply, "Lord help me."

Immediately, after I cried out to God, an overwhelming sense of fatigue came over me. I calmed down and I went to bed. The next morning I woke to the same existing issues, but I had a fresh, new outlook. I was ready to walk forward and never look back. It still baffles me I ever considered going back to that unhealthy relationship.

Over time, I did learn to love God in ways I sought after in men. I drew closer and closer to Him through a consistent prayer life and bible study. I began to understand what a "true" love relationship was like. I learned it could sustain you through anything. I started early detecting situations that were unhealthy for me to be in (I will speak more about this concept later). For each of us to be cancer free in the area of relationships, we must continuously pray for discernment and use it when God gives it to us - noticing the warning signs, and staying very determined to treat abnormal conditions in our lives before they have a chance to do major damage.

Walking in my Healing

As I moved forward, finding a new job and relocating back to my college home town to garner the support of friends, I received a call from this same person who had sold most of my possessions, threatened my life and even rejected my return to him. He was ranting about having messed up again – smoking crack, selling his car, and feeling hopeless and desperate. In my previous condition, I would have been quick to respond by wiring money or taking some other codependent action.

Take note that I was never nasty and never felt led to repay evil for evil. I offered him encouragement that as long as he still had a job and the city had public transportation, he had an opportunity to make good on his mistake. I offered him prayer. He never called again.

Once re-established in my college town, I met a guy, who was a friend of a friend. I had learned enough to ask a few questions on the onset. The friend gave the okay to share my number but looking back he seemed to have some reservation. This gentleman called me late that evening and in our getting to know each other, I asked, "So what church do you attend?" His response, "Religion is cool if that's your thing. I'm not into all of that." From what I had gathered he was a pretty nice guy with a pretty good job. However, he was missing something that had become very important to me - a relationship with the Lord. In my previous condition, I would have seen this as an opportunity to "minister" to him in hopes he would worship with me and come to know the Lord, and perhaps we would live happily ever after. I was walking in my healing in the area of relationships. In total contrast to my 18-year pattern, I politely informed him I would be blocking his number as soon as the call was over. His response, "Hey, what do you know? You may be the one to change me." Being cancer free in this area, I knew quite clear that was something only God could do!

Abnormalities in the Workplace

I spent 23 years in an Accounting career. Reflecting back over the time, I consider every bit of it a struggle. Struggle is defined as a forceful attempt to get free of restraint or resist attack. It also involves contending with an adversary or opposing force.

Within the last five of those 23 years, I reached a point where I became very bitter in my workplace. Much like the effects of physical cancer, I did not care what was torn down or who was affected. I simply wanted to be cancer in my workplace. I was tired of hearing someone else was more qualified than I was, and that is why he or she was promoted. I was tired of watching other people build the lives they dreamed of for themselves and their families. I could no longer take hearing, "You make good money, so you should just be satisfied to be here."

I was always viewed as a leader in my work groups. I had been noted as a "person of influence" as well. With the condition of bitterness, being a person of influence became counterproductive to a work group. It made for some interesting dynamics in the office. Those who still had hopes that promotion would not pass them by were quick to disassociate themselves with me, assuming that mere association would disqualify them, as had been my plight.

I no longer desired to go the extra mile. I had no real motivation to do so. I knew many other employees were looking to me for guidance and leadership but I was unable to provide much in this condition. I wanted to show the other minorities that upward mobility was possible, but somehow I could not shatter the glass ceiling.

My time never came, and I felt trapped. I did not wreak havoc because that is not the kind of person I am. I just struggled to hide my feelings of disappointment and grief and continue to be a light to others. It felt as though my hopes for a progressively rewarding career were snuffed out. I spent a lot of energy discussing my plight with others. Often times, they could not support me in this condition. I prayed and tried to be content. I asked God if this was the place for me, then help me to find peace in the midst. It never came.

I am generally a very happy and uplifting person. It is who I am at the very core of my being, and that part of me had been infected by the cancer of bitterness. Unfortunately, this was a cancer that easily spread and affected everyone around me at work and at home.

What is Your Condition?

Perhaps you are saying, "I've not had either of those conditions." I encourage you to reexamine the definition of cancer, cells, and tissues before concluding you are cancer free. A few other conditions I have observed are:

- The family member who shows up for every family function and always manages to sow discord due to unresolved issues of the past
- The church member who joins with the agenda of finding a husband or wife at any cost with no regard for relationships that have already been established, not excluding the pastor
- The church member who refuses to support the pastor and works hard to develop a team of supporters to always

reject the pastor's vision

- The woman who seeks out male support of any kind at any cost because she is unwilling to trust God to provide for her and her family

- The man who continues to manipulate women by telling them what they want to hear long enough to get what he wants and until he wants something else.

- The coworker who works to sabotage the efforts of others

- The company who hires the top available candidates but fails to provide them with an objective playing field for advancement and promotion

- The member of the political, social or civic group who refuses to work with the collective body to accomplish the mission of the group

- The member of any group, family, church, work, political, civic or social who always displays a negative disposition creating an unpleasant environment for all in their presence.

These are just a few illustrations of cancerous conditions that exist. In the examples where gender has been highlighted, I am confident the roles could be easily reversed. These conditions eat away at the very core of the team, group, family or other collective unit to which they belong. Their staggering effects often result in death-death of quality family structure, death of marriages and relationships, death of churches, death of motivation and active engagement in the workplace, death of progression in social and civic activities.

Early Detection & Self-Examination

With cancer, you must begin with a baseline of what is normal. When you touch or detect something that feels abnormal, you can act quickly to have it examined further. If I'd taken the time to establish what was "right" in a relationship and evaluate what was "wrong" with my choices earlier in my dating life, then some of the patterns could have been altered earlier so that I ceased to make the same reckless decisions or at a minimum early detected behaviors that didn't line up with what I would have established as normal and healthy.

I should have left my job sooner. I should not have stayed around for rejection after rejection. I should have been okay with moving on. When I look at some of the factors, which cause breast cancer including stress, I realize the stress that came from staying in an unhealthy work environment may have been a contributing factor in my development of breast cancer.

Relapses

I caution you to remember all cancers maintain a potential for recurrence or relapse. Deliverance and healing are a continuous process.

Sometimes life has a way of zapping your energy and will to do what is right. So even after you know what is right, there exists a potential to revert back to old, unhealthy and destructive habits. Relapses occur when you do not maintain the proper accountability and convince yourself you can manage your condition alone.

In cancer of the body, this is a recurrence of cells acting abnormally. In every other area of our lives, this is a recurrence of destructive patterns that run the risk of affecting every other aspect of our being.

{3}

WHAT IS YOUR TREAMENT PLAN?

What a quick turn of events! My treatment plan changed from simple to aggressive in just a few short weeks. Even before finding the tumor in my lymph node, my breast surgeon recommended chemotherapy based on the pathology of the cells from my first surgery. He said on a scale of 1 to 3, my cell grade was 3 or high grade. This means my abnormal cells looked very different from my normal cells. These cells grow quickly in a disorganized and irregular pattern to divide and make new cancer cells. My mitoses, HER2 status and other pathology revealed a very aggressive cancer was growing inside of me. I was upgraded from stage 0 to stage 2A.

Once I obtained and met my oncologist, he told me that, in his more than 20 years of medical practice, a mitotic count of 40/10 high power fields (HPF) was one of the highest he had observed. That number is an indication how rapidly the cells were dividing. It became very clear to me that these abnormal cells were acting reckless in my body. With all of the new findings, my treatment plan had to change. I had the second surgery two weeks after the first, and just two weeks after the second surgery, I began chemotherapy.

During my second surgery, I also had a portacath (port) put in for ease of receiving the chemotherapy into my body. At this point in my journey, there was not a lot of delaying, we trekked full steam ahead.

Just before chemotherapy began, a position emission tomography (PET) scan was performed which identified that no active cancer was present in my body. The chemotherapy and radiation were still a part of my treatment plan to prevent recurrence.

Chemotherapy

I had eight doses of ACT Chemotherapy. "ACT" stands for **A**-Adriamycin **C**-Cytoxan, **T**-Taxol. The **AC** combination was given in the first four treatments and the **T** was given in the final four or second set of treatments (chemocare.com). Chemotherapy is intended to attack any fast growing cells. The cells that are fast growing in our bodies are our white blood cells, hair cells, and cancer cells. That is why when a person gets chemotherapy, their immune systems are negatively affected and they potentially have hair loss because their white blood cells and hair cells are being destroyed along with the cancer cells. The job of the chemotherapy is to destroy anything with the same fast growing and moving characteristics as the cancer cells.

My chemotherapy took 16 weeks total. I would go for treatment on a Wednesday, start experiencing the side effects and feel really bad by Friday, and begin to feel better the following Monday or Tuesday. I would have a week in between my treatments for my body to rest, heal and start the process all over again.

Radiation

Radiation works differently. It heavily targets the "infected" area by damaging the DNA of cancerous tissue leading to cellular death. It focuses only on the initial problem area. I had radiation treatments five days a week for seven weeks. I had a few more complications with radiation than I did with chemotherapy. Going every day was taxing for me, and seeing the effects that it had on my body and the other patients too was mentally challenging as well. I will spare you the specific details of the experience, but let me just say that radiation can burn through skin.

I was able to return to work while going through radiation. It is powerful, but it was not time consuming. I would drive myself to the treatments and then drive back to work because the process only took about 15 minutes. I will admit this was one of the hardest parts of journey for me. I was a lot more emotional during this process.

I am still on Tamoxifen, the 5 year pill. Wikipedia states that Tamoxifen acts like a key broken off in a lock that prevents any other key from being inserted, preventing estrogen from binding to its receptor. Hence, breast cancer cell growth is blocked.

Other Treatments

My physical body was not the only part of me being treated. My entire being was going through a transformation. I say my soul (fully encompassing my mind, will and emotions) and spirit were experiencing chemotherapy and radiation as well.

I took full advantage of the time between chemotherapy treatments. Every moment I felt up to it, I took the time to nourish my spirit. I would read and listen to praise and worship tapes that warmed my heart and encouraged my soul. I would also study Scriptures on healing. I drew most of my strength from these precious times. I was determined to win the battles of doubt and fear that desired to invade my mind, and the only way I knew to do that was to use the tools on which my foundation had been built.

I had reconciled that God was not the orchestrator of my cancer. I do not believe that God is the author of sickness, but I do believe that nothing can happen to us that He does not allow. I had already decided from the beginning my journey was a win-win and that it would be victorious regardless of the outcome. I had accepted Christ in my life and I had already begun a relationship with Him. Looking back, I realize this journey drew me even closer to Him.

The praise and worship music was like chemotherapy, flowing through my entire being, attacking every attempt of the Satan to find a resting place within my soul and spirit. Specific scriptures relating to faith and healing were like radiation, powerfully targeting any direct attacks on my faith. Listed below are a just a few scriptures I relied on daily throughout this journey.

Psalm 34:19 *"Many are the afflictions of the righteous: but the Lord delivereth him out of them all."*

Psalm 91:11 *"For he shall give his angels charge over thee, to keep thee in all thy ways."*

2 Corinthians 4:16 *"For which cause we faint not; but though our outward man perish, yet the inward man is renewed day by day."*

Philippians 4:6 *"Be careful for nothing; but in every thing by prayer and supplication with thanksgiving let your requests be made known unto God."*

Mark 5:34 *"And he said unto her, Daughter, thy faith hath made thee whole; go in peace, and be whole of thy plague."*

Don't Trade Cancer for Cancer

I want to mention that the potential is high to trade one cancerous condition for another. With each failed relationship, I could easily have hated all men and labeled them as being dogs. Instead, I chose to look at myself, digging deep to see what it was that caused me to continue to accept these patterns in my life. Once I learned more about myself, I came to grips with the realization that I was trying to compensate as an adult for the male affection I did not receive as a child. People think that women who have those kinds of problems grew up fatherless. I was blessed to live in a two-parent home, and my father loved me.

My father was a great provider, disciplinarian, educator, civil rights leader and church leader. I realized that although he loved me the best way that he knew how, something was missing. Back then, my father worked a lot and did not have much time to spend with me. I believe this was a major reason why I allowed the companionship of men who were needy and in many ways dependent on me.

Getting to the root cause of my past relationship issues helped me to seek the proper treatment for this issue. First, I prayed and asked God to give me what I was seeking, not in someone else but in Him. Secondly, I spent time reading books that gave me courage and hope and showed me the benefits of being single, whole and healed from past mistakes.

My father and I have a great relationship and we love each other. I understand that he is human. The more I learn about my family, the more I realize my dad had his own life experiences that shaped his methods of parenting. There are people who would choose to create an additional cancerous condition by blaming their fathers or other family members for their shortcomings. As a result, they fail to nurture and grow the relationship with the precious time remaining or spend the rest of their lives being bitter.

I do not think I have ever really had this conversation with my dad. I never talked to my father about it because it was not required for my treatment. The easiest thing for me to do was to acknowledge why I allowed the abnormalities to exist, accept responsibility for the choices I made as a result, and forgive my dad and myself. My dad is still in my life and we actively work on our relationship. As a result I am cancer free in this area. The forgiveness process was an integral part of my individual treatment plan. The cancerous condition continues to exist with the person that chooses not to forgive.

Forgiveness does not require you to have a daily interaction with someone. It just means you are not carrying around bitterness and baggage that affects your ability to have healthy and meaningful relationships with others.

Beauty Treatments

At every moment of our lives we experience emotions and reactions to life's challenges and constant changes. God has gifted us with our emotions so we should not feel guilty for whatever our current state may be. Just noticing where you are and how you are feeling will help you assess the health of your present state and give you clarity on steps you can take to get to a healthier, more desirable place. If your desired place is one of healing and wholeness, you will be more willing to seek the treatment you need to get there.

Please recognize that although your cancerous journey may affect others, the choice of treatment is personal. Individuals must decide for themselves what they are willing to sacrifice or go through to get there. Understand that the choice not to treat your condition is an option. However, be clear this option almost always leads to death in some form. It may be days, months or years, but death is bound to occur.

There is a beauty in getting diagnosed with any condition. That beauty is the ability to treat it. Treatment is a choice. It is not easy, but it is worth it. Unfortunately, there are some who choose to go through their entire lives always plagued with issues that bind them and keep them from fulfilling their life's purpose.

{4}

WHO IS YOUR SUPPORT SYSTEM?

During my treatment period, my extended family, friends, church family, coworkers and others took great care of my husband, my daughter and me. I believe one of the reasons I had such a great support system was my willingness to be open about my condition. There are so many things to consider when you are going through the process. I am a wife and a mother and I had a household to keep in order. There were varying roles that had to continue. When it came to the care of my daughter, who was only two years old at the time, I insisted my mother make that her full time responsibility. I did not want my daughter to be tossed around from caregiver to caregiver. Even though, I too was in need of a caregiver and understandably, my mom was my first choice, I knew I would rest better knowing that most of her efforts would be focused on my little angel.

I enlisted early on the help of my prayer partner and friend to be my caregiver after each treatment. She stayed during the three nights immediately after each treatment. That was her consistent role. Another one of my dear friends volunteered to take me to each treatment. She worked from home so she had the ability to continue to work during my treatments.

One of the great things about having a wonderful support system is that no one was overburdened. The reality is that even though this period was an intense time in my life, the people who supported me still had their own lives with which to contend. When I look back on it now, if I had overburdened my mother with taking care of my daughter, getting me to all of my appointments, and coming to maintain my house, it would have been too much. It was nice to have different people designated for different things.

My husband did a lot of the cooking. Another thing he did to maintain a sense of normalcy for our daughter was faithfully take her to church every Sunday. My daughter loved it because she was a huge fan of the choir and because of the energy she experienced from the worship music. I made a conscious decision to stay out of large crowds, including church, due to the state of my immune system. My church sent me DVDs of the Sunday services and when our church began streaming the service live on Sundays, I was able to watch from home even while lying in bed.

When my husband was in town he also did a lot of chores around the house. He did not have a direct role in my treatments or the side effects associated with them. I am going to talk about this more a little later in this chapter.

My co-workers got together and decided what days they would bring dinner to the house. This made all the difference in the world, not only for me, but also for my family and those who had taken on various roles in my caregiving. My boss and I shared a healthy cookbook. She would have me pick out a recipe from the book and on every other Sunday she would cook my selection and bring it to the house.

There were other church family members with children my daughter's age that would come by and pick her up so that she could play at their house or go with them to events that I was unable to attend during this season. This played a huge part in giving my daughter a sense of normalcy too.

So as you can see, having a huge support system helped to normalize my chaotic life. I even had someone who provided me with a housecleaning service. That was huge because I was able to come home after treatments to a clean environment. I am confident that a lot of these actions of others influenced how I faired through the process.

I know that people have different reasons for keeping their diagnosis to themselves but I believe a great support system is key. I am now more sensitive and proactive about playing a role in other's support when I learn of their cancer diagnosis. Some of the help I found that cancer patients need most are transportation to and from doctor's appointments, housecleaning, and help purchasing food and supplements that best support them during treatment.

You Have Not Because You Ask Not

I encourage you to ask for help. Whether your challenge is a physical cancer or another cancerous condition that threatens to tear down the very essence of your being, do not try to go through it alone. There are people who are willing to help. Sometimes those people exist beyond the boundaries of your normal comfort zone.

Furthermore, do not place specific expectations on certain people. In other words, do not expect certain people to do specific things because of who they are in your life. In my situation, I learned that it was hard for my husband to come in real close to the physical aspects of my situation. I am referring to actually participating in my treatment and watching me experience the side effects.

I remember asking him at one particular instance to go with me to a doctor's appointment and him getting physically ill. He could not come out of the bathroom and I ended up having to leave him because time for my appointment was drawing near. All he could do was apologize.

Another time when I was in my second set of chemotherapy, I was hurting really badly and I asked him to help me by rubbing my legs. He said, "I'm getting ready to go cut the grass." Now, I know my husband well enough to know that he is not an insensitive person. I had to realize that it was too much for him. His cutting the grass was his contribution. He was maintaining the house for me, and doing what he knew to do.

What was interesting was when I called my prayer partner and told her what I was experiencing, she asked me what she could do. I told her that I had read about other cancer patients walking during this treatment, and she came right away to take me to a park where we could walk through the pain. I remember so vividly the look on my husband's face as we were pulling out of the driveway. It was a look of intense sadness on his face. I believe he was sorry that he could not do more.

I had someone who questioned me about my husband's lack of involvement from their perspective. Even my oncologist inquired once as to how we were doing through this process. He noted that he had not seen him at any of my appointments and he highlighted the fact that many marriages do not make it through these types of trials. Spouses vow to be there in sickness and in health but when sickness becomes a reality, some spouses flee. I informed him that I had made peace with the role my husband seemed able to play. I had come to realize that there were certain parts of my journey that he just could not handle.

I did not place any additional strain on the marriage by forcing him to play roles he seemed incapable of playing regardless of my opinion or the opinion of others. To the average person it would seem that he should have been able to do anything I asked of him. It would have been different for me if my husband was not supportive at all or if I felt like he had no interest and did not care. That was not the case and I never got that feeling from him.

What my husband could and could not handle was very apparent. I did not try to inflict a deeper or closer role on him. I allowed him to be what he could be. I think that is important for you to understand. Even when you are going through the other cancerous conditions, there is a tendency to expect certain persons to play pivotal roles in your healing process. That is a very limiting belief. Remember your ultimate goal is to be healed.

Trust that there are people in your life who are willing and capable to help you. Where you feel those people do not currently exist, be willing to speak up and do what is necessary to get the support you need. The goal is to be healed. Part of being present with your condition is accepting other people's limitations. When I noticed people's limitations, I did not try to force them to play a role that stretched them beyond their limitations. The reality is that people get to choose how they want to help you. Your progress is more successful when you are willing to ask for what you need even if it requires stepping outside your comfort zone.

I understood what support I had and what I did not have. I purposely did not overburden any one person in an attempt to keep my resources within safe and familiar boundaries. I was blessed to have a tremendous support system. I know this may not be everyone's norm. I am a very giving person and I believe what scripture says concerning the reaping of seeds you have sown. The giving I did to others had come back to me, and I was in awe.

Some people have asked me about the art of receiving help. It may sound silly but some people just do not know how to accept help!

When people ask them what they need, they say "nothing," even when they are in dire need of help.

It may be playing it safe to say 'no' when an offer to help is made. Perhaps your past experiences have caused you to believe that all offers come with a price that must be paid. Therefore, whether you have realistically determined that the answer to the question "Can I really do this by myself" is no and the answer to the question "Would it not be easier to have the help" is yes, you still attempt to get through it alone. Unfortunately, this means you may not get the desired results or that it may take you longer than necessary to get them. It could mean that time runs out on you before you get your healing. You stretch yourself too thin and create additional conditions by not asking for help and accepting available support.

Why do we struggle with getting the support we need? I think it is because it requires building trust in relationships. Relationships are simply interactions with people. Some are deep, personal, and loving. Other relationships are strictly business and others are mere acts of service.

Consider the reservations you have that trick you into believing you are safer and will be successful in isolation. When you are in isolation, you are in your most vulnerable place. You have no one to help you fight, you are weak and you are left open to attacks. Satan can play with your head and feed you thoughts of defeat. You will not have anyone to encourage you and offer you the hope and support you desperately need if you keep yourself in that place.

I encourage you to reach out and give someone an opportunity to help you. You may be surprised with the help and resources that come your way. You do run the risk of being vulnerable with people, however to get something you have never had, you have to do something you have never done. It is time for you to step outside of your comfort zone.

Having so many people in and out of my home was very different and letting my child go places with people for the first time was difficult. Let me be clear, there were some people who offered to help in ways that I declined, especially when it involved my child. I know that people had the best of intentions, but this was another area where the gift of discernment was extremely important.

In order to maintain your health and to heal continuously from any cancer or addiction, you have to have people in your life that will support you in your treatment and recovery. When you are ready to be made whole, God will provide everyone and everything you need to aid you in the process. He anxiously awaits your surrender but God will never force His way into your life. When you ask Him, He will provide for you. You have to trust that the support you need will come. Opening yourself up to receiving help is one of the best gifts you can give to yourself as you seek to be healed.

Pay it Forward

Do not get so self-absorbed that you forget the people who love and care for you. As I mentioned previously, the caregivers and other people in your life are still experiencing their own trials and tribulations. I encourage you to remember their support and make sure you give back.

Everything was not about me when I was going through my cancer journey. I can remember coming home from a treatment and my mom needing a shoulder to cry on because of some things that were going on in her personal life. I was not able to do much, but I could listen, and that is what I did. Yes my cancer was life threatening but from my perspective so are all the other conditions that exist. Even in the midst of our challenges we have to take the time to see if our support system needs anything from us that we can provide.

{5}

SIDE EFFECTS

The major side effect of the AC chemotherapy combination was extreme nausea. I would actually be infused with two bags of nausea medication before the chemotherapy was even started. In addition to that, I would get a prescription of two pills and a full bottle of a less powerful nausea medication to take home. The only way for me to combat the nausea was to try to sleep through it. Even with all of the medications, there was nothing that completely eliminated it.

When the nausea began to subside, and I felt up to eating, I still had other struggles because my taste buds had altered. I remember waking up one morning and craving breakfast from McDonalds. One of my friends was eager to bring it to me. She was excited that I had an appetite. I remember the aroma of the hot cakes and sausage and I could not wait to dig in. I experienced a great let down as I anticipated a familiar taste that presently did not exist.

The nurse who administered my chemotherapy informed me during my first visit to the clinic that with the AC combination I was guaranteed hair loss. This was only concerning to me because my daughter had been accustomed to playing and pulling on my hair. I worried about my hair falling out in clumps as she was playing, so I decided to be proactive. One Sunday after church my husband, daughter and I gathered together in our bathroom, and my husband cut my hair as short as possible. I can still remember my daughter in her little innocent voice, "Daddy why you do dat to Mommy?" By the completion of my second treatment, my hair-all of my hair-was completely gone.

I had tremendous joint pain with the Taxol treatment. It would be virtually impossible for me to lay still for the first few days after the Taxol treatment. My doctor prescribed Percocet to combat the pain, but I preferred not to take it. I researched and learned that constant walking had helped countless others who preferred not to rely on narcotics for pain management. While I could not realistically walk 24 hours a day, walking to combat the side effects of the pain became a regimen I continue even today. What was previously a means to pain management has now become a means for me and a team of others to raise money for breast cancer research and treatment for others.

As for the hair loss, I purchased pretty scarves, hats decorated with jewelry, and fashionable wigs, the latter of which I ended up not wearing. In an effort to be proactive, I purchased the wigs before I even began treatment. The first time I tried a wig on at home my daughter cried and broke out in a sweat. Therefore, I took it off just to comfort her and vowed not to wear it. Once my hair fell out completely, I found that I liked the way I looked. I maintained this look except for my time at the cancer clinic. Often times, the treatment rooms were so cold that I felt I needed to wear a hat since my immune system was already being compromised. I wore very fashionable hats. I had to keep it cute. Two of my favorites were a pink hat with lovely jewelry on it and a brown hat with a big pretty bow on the right side of it.

Early in my cancer journey, I met a woman in McDonalds. I met her on a day when I was having a rough time processing my diagnosis. I was only there in an effort to appease my daughter who already seemed to sense that change was coming. I intended to talk to no one but as it turned out, this woman and her grandchildren were in the booth next to us. My daughter was determined to interact with them. I am typically a very friendly and open person so trying to keep my distance took quite a bit of effort for me. I finally opened up to her about my condition and as it turned out she was a cancer research nurse for the clinic I would be attending. We struck up a wonderful conversation and she encouraged me "Every day you wake up, you get up, you look up, and you dress up, even when you don't feel like it." That message was so profound, and I realized how much of a therapy it was for other people when I took that approach. Therefore, I always went to the treatment facility looking my best, regardless of how I felt.

I kept up with fashion trends, ensuring my hats and clothes always looked nice. The other patients would perk up when they saw me. Some of them would make comments like, "You always wear the prettiest hats." I brought energy, liveliness, and hope to the treatment facility. It was my choice to be present with my situation and go there with a positive attitude. Just because I felt bad did not mean that I had to look bad. It not only helped me, it helped others.

Side Effects of Cancerous Conditions

A major side effect of my choices in relationships was low self-esteem. Over time, I began to doubt my own self-worth and as a result, I continued to make bad choices and repeat the same unhealthy behaviors.

There has been some research, which suggests that bitterness negatively impacts a person's physical health. A study performed by psychologist Dr. Carsten Wrosch suggests when a person harbors bitterness for a long time, they may experience impairments in their metabolism, immune response and organ function as well as experience physical disease."

There are side effects to every cancerous condition we face in our lives. Some refer to the side effects of low self-esteem and bitterness as epidemics with far-reaching consequences to the mental and physical body.

Side Effects of Treatment

Whether you experience hair loss from chemotherapy or the

beginning of self-love after years of low self-esteem, there is a definite transformation process that results from the treatment. This transformation is the commonality that exists. Ironically, the evidence of the transformation that takes place with treatment of the physical vs other cancerous conditions is in complete contrast.

As I mentioned through the sharing of my own experience with breast cancer, side effects of chemotherapy and radiation can be grueling on the body, painful and tough to manage. For some, hair loss causes them a lot of mental anguish.

The opposite is true of the transformation that takes place in the life of the person who is willing to be treated for conditions like those illustrated in Chapter 2, which depict greed, selfishness, envy, hatred and un-forgiveness. For these and other destructive agents that invade us and threaten to destroy us, the evident side effects of getting treated are refreshing in the least. Some results that can be expected are self-love, selflessness, unselfishness, love and respect for others. For those willing to go through the process required for change, the effects include the freedom and opportunity to become the person God intended and fashioned you to be.

{6}

HOW DO YOU LIVE IN SURVIVORVILLE?

Birthdays are generally a special time of celebration for most people. Traditionally, cancer survivors who cherish survivorship celebrate two birthdays. They celebrate the day they were born, and the day they were diagnosed with cancer, called their "survivor" date. In addition to my birthday in March, I celebrate December 20th each year.

A survivor is "a person who survives, especially a person remaining alive after an event in which others have died." I am fully aware that if a person is breathing and talking, they are considered to be alive. Looking at this concept a little deeper, I ask how alive are you? Are you thriving or merely existing?

I urge you not to limit yourself to a simple existence. Overcoming trials and living in victory is a process that requires you to broaden your view about them. If you look closely with an open mind, you will see benefits and blessings to what you have experienced.

When you share your story of what you have overcome, share it from a place of triumph so that others can receive encouragement from you. Remember, battle begins in the mind. Your fight is not just getting treatment for your cancer and getting cured. It is a continuous battle. As a survivor, you are the evidence that all things are possible.

Before your cancerous condition, did you have dreams or aspirations? When you dig deeply, you will discover you still have things about which you are passionate. Do not allow your desires to become dormant because your mind tells you that you are no longer able to pursue them. As long as you have life, you have endless possibilities.

I admonish you to live your dreams. You are still alive, you still have breath in your body, and you still have the opportunity to allow those dreams and those goals to come alive for you. This is not just for your benefit, but it is for you to be of service to others.

I took a personal development class once and had a rather interesting yet unusual experience. During introductions, I shared that I had had cancer. I believe something about the way I discussed it may have indicated to the facilitators this was something I considered to be a flaw.

One part of the course involved individualized assignments aimed at strengthening character in each participant. My assignment was to go stand on a street corner, and do two things. I had to make eye contact with everyone that passed by me, and only say to them, "I'm a survivor." I could not answer any questions they had; I could only say, "I'm a survivor."

Talk about awkward! It felt so weird at first, but doing this became easier as the time passed. I reflected on just how much of a survivor I had been throughout my entire life. I began to have flashbacks of other situations that I had overcome.

On February 22, 1991, while attending college, I was held at gunpoint at an ATM machine. It was a terribly traumatic experience that happened in broad daylight. It is a long story, but my robber actually ended up in my car. I learned from this experience that once a person gets into your head, they can control you in any kind of way. There was another man coming into the building where I was being held up. I wanted to say something but the robber threatened, "I have enough bullets for both of you. We're going to act like we're together, and we're going to leave." So we left, I let him in my car, and we went up the street to another bank. He made me park right in front of the building and told me to roll my window down so that he could have direct aim at me, just in case I tried to run or do anything he considered "stupid."

Through a course of interrogations, it was determined this armed robber had held up several women in an every other day pattern. When he was apprehended, he had a loaded .45 and a crack pipe on him. I am convinced that he needed the money and was not in a stable state of mind. I cannot help but consider if I had done anything contrary to what he had requested, I might not be alive today.

The armed robbery, violent past relationships, and, of course, breast cancer were the three major things that came to memory as I reflected on being a survivor. Looking back, I realized I have survived this and so much more.

My faith has kept me through a lot of situations. Even in times when I did not walk in my survivorship with a heart of gratitude, it was that foundation that reminded me that through it all, I had learned to trust and depend on God.

Real victory comes more from knowing that a greater purpose exists than simply being able to say, "I made it." We do not overcome or get deliverance just for the sake of gaining a new title, "survivor", "overcomer", or "conqueror".

When you look back at the definition of a survivor, that last part says,"...especially a person remaining alive after an event in which others have died." Stay positive and take pride in being a survivor. Understand that surviving is more than just being here. It includes knowing your assignment is not over here on Earth.

Overcoming by the Word of our Testimony

While writing this book, I was struggling with the idea of sharing a subsequent condition that arose since my bout with breast cancer. I decided it was important to share it as it shows that staying in a place of healing is work and a continuous process.

Immediately after my cancer journey, there was a period where my husband and I were not in sync. I was trying to live my life to fullest. I walked around with my "new" short hair with dignity and pride. I was in my zone. However, we as a team seemed to be growing apart.

A part of me thinks that he could have been operating from a place of fear although we never discussed it. I am sure it was not easy watching me go through my breast cancer journey. Perhaps he wondered if I was going to live or die. Some people hold on with all of their might to the point of smothering their partner in situations like these, while others let go and move on because they are afraid love will be lost in the process anyway. My husband's actions seemed to resemble more of the latter.

This was a very lonely and difficult time for me. I found myself in a battle mentally. The compliments and encouragements I wanted from my husband started to come from other places. It was not easy to turn away from these potentially unhealthy situations. Would you not know it—traits of a cancerous condition had shown up in my desire for affirmation and support.

It was a fight to do the right thing. I early detected abnormal thoughts and behaviors I was experiencing. I maintained accountability with a dear friend. I prayed and asked God to help me. I made choices that supported my greater desire to be pleasing in God's eyes. I am confident I survived this season because of my faith in and relationship with God. I had memorized 1 Corinthians 10:13 which reminded me that *"There hath no temptation taken you but such as is common to man: but God is faithful, who will not suffer you to be tempted above that ye are able; but will with the temptation also make a way to escape, that ye may be able to bear it."*

With all that I had been through and all that God had kept me through I never expected a condition to show up that had the potential to negatively affect my marriage.

I share this to emphasize, when we least expect them, cancerous conditions show up and attempt to take root. They are not foreign substances that invade us. They are the normal parts of us-the emotions and desires-that begin acting abnormal. We should always give consideration to how our emotions and desires affect others. We all have the potential to become cancerous in our circles of influence. I thank God that I better understand how situations like these arise. I thank Him even more that His word provides what we need to overcome any situation.

Getting through the rough times goes back to choice. I have emphasized throughout this book that we are sometimes required to make tough and painful choices to be treated. Survival often depends on our willingness to go through uncomfortable and excruciating processes. Once you've survived, your experience becomes your testimony and positions you to encourage someone else.

{7}

WHOSE REPORT WILL YOU BELIEVE?

The PET scan I had just before I started chemotherapy involved drinking a sugar substance, and sitting for a while, to allow the substance to spread through my body. The sugar binds to recognizable cancerous cells and highlights them. This scan was necessary since my second surgery identified tumors in my lymph nodes. The doctors were checking to see if the cancer had spread to any other places in my body.

The results came back and showed that there was no active cancer present in my body. I was still set to receive chemotherapy and radiation to prevent recurrence. With much of this journey still in front of me, there was the potential to doubt all the doctors were saying.

I pose this question to you, "Whose report do you believe?" When God, the doctor or other persons of authority have spoken over you and announced your healing, are you going to believe them or are you going to believe the lie that Satan is speaking? Once you've been told that you're healed, free, and delivered are you going to walk in your healing or are you going to still be weighed down by the cares, fears and worries of the condition you've been delivered from?

One day I walked into my doctor's office and I was having a moment of anxiety. I asked him what the chances were of my breast cancer coming back. My doctor replied with life changing words that I now live by. He said to me, "Dywuana, we gave you the most aggressive treatment that we could give you so you could live. Now go and live." From that day forward, I decided that I was not going to look back to "what ifs" as they could only be bondage for me and prevent me from walking in total healing, which was the report I had received.

Healing in definition is pretty simple. It means to be made healthy again, to restore to health, or to be free from ailment. A lot of times we will say that we are healed, but we still find ourselves acting in a way that speaks a different truth.

Unfortunately other people may continue to view you or label you with the condition you once had, even when you are in your place of healing. Refuse to allow them to use what you have been through to keep you down or held hostage. Always be determined that the past is behind you. If you choose to use past conditions as messages, campaigns or programs to help others that is awesome.

Sometimes you have to disconnect with people who seem to operate only in negative reporting, especially when they are not the authority. It doesn't mean you love them any less, it just means you're making choices to better align with the report of authority you've been given.

I have had to check myself on plenty of occasions and make sure that I do not allow others to aid me in recreating old patterns. I refuse to have a relapse or recurrence of cancerous conditions I have power to remain free from. I must confidently walk in my healing. I have to continue to speak positively over my life and to make good choices. I encourage you to do the same.

Signs

There should be signs of your healing and wholeness. One key to remember is that thoughts are a choice. What you choose to create in your mind, you create in your life. Scripture is very clear, the transformation that we desire in our lives begins with the renewal of our minds (Romans 12:2). When you are confident about the things you feel about yourself and more importantly confident about what scripture says about you, you are properly armed to overcome anything.

Healing is a process. Even a minor cut of the finger goes through a process of healing. Sometimes if the cut is deep enough or severe enough it can cause permanent scarring. Scars should not be viewed as negative but rather as additional evidence of your victory over your circumstance. Four scars I have from breast cancer are the discoloration of skin from the radiation burns, a 2 inch scar where my port was placed, two small scars-one from the lumpectomy and the other from the lymph node removal.

Choose to view every situation positively. Realize that when opportunities seem to pass you by, God may be protecting you or have something better planned for you. I am a personal testament to this. I was extremely bitter about my lack of promotion. I did not take the positive road and my peace of mind and health suffered for it. Looking back, I realized that life may have been easier for me, had I looked at my circumstances differently.

Live fully the life you have been given. Make the most of every opportunity and stop looking back. There is a difference between looking back and glancing back. Glancing back is okay because you get to see how far you have come. When you glance back, you still have the ability to move forward. However, keeping your head turned back will prevent you from moving forward. It may create a longing for the past and that is not good especially if that is not where you are supposed to be.

Your mind will try to convince you your past is better than where you are headed. That is just not true because the best is yet to come. Job 8:7 states *"Though thy beginning was small, yet thy latter end should greatly increase."* and Haggai 2:9 affirms *"The glory of this latter house shall be greater than of the former, saith the Lord of hosts: and in this place will I give peace, saith the Lord of hosts."* Both verses assure us that our latter days will be greater than our former ones.

I have learned you can change your limiting beliefs by creating new neural-pathways, or mindsets and ways of thinking. You can do this in a variety of ways including creating vision boards, journaling, reading, attending personal development and church conferences, and watching these types of events online. These avenues allow you to see and experience new things. Van Moody, Pastor of the Worship Center Christian Church in Birmingham, Alabama and author of "The People Factor" said once, "You can't think higher than what you've been exposed to." I cannot agree more.

When I learned through studying the word of God that there was no good thing God would withhold from me if I walked uprightly (Psalm 84:11), I realized that what I was not getting was not good for me. Standing firm on my faith and daily affirming the truths of God's word through the Bible and the messages and teachings of other godly influences, are important routines that have sustained me through some very difficult times.

I go back now and look at my journals. I have journaled for a huge portion of my life, although I have not been entirely consistent with it. I encourage people to journal and to use daily affirmations. You can write down and meditate on scriptures that directly pertain to your current situation or condition. You can also write quotes that you hear and feel support your healing. I encourage you to write down your thoughts whether you are in a positive or negative state of mind. When you do not have the strength to get through your current situations, you can refer back to your journal and see other things you have written to inspire you or other times you felt this way and witnessed God's deliverance. Journaling helps you reaffirm your thoughts and desires of healing. There is something very special about reading your own encouragements. It serves as a reminder that victory and healing are available for you.

{8}

WHY ARE YOU HERE?

While there are so many statistics of those who have survived breast cancer and other cancers, there are still numerous statistics of those who have not. One of the greatest inspirations I have for walking in the Susan G. Komen 3-day 60 mile walk is the memorial service that is held during the opening ceremony to honor those who have finished their race in the fight against breast cancer. A flag is displayed listing the names of family and friends and at the designated time waved in their honor.

My grandmother and I battled breast cancer at the same time; she was diagnosed with breast cancer almost 6 months before I was. It was really a tough time for my dad to go through this journey with my grandmother and me at the same time.

At the age of 94, my grandmother opted to receive radiation only and completed her treatments just shortly before I was diagnosed. It was interesting how she would call me and coach me through chemotherapy even though she had not actually gone through it. She wanted to make sure that I was okay. She seemed to be relieved that I made it through my chemo so well. I suspect she had not considered the advances made in chemotherapy over the years of her life. Nevertheless it seemed that as soon as I completed that phase of my treatment, she began to decline. The day after my last chemotherapy, my grandmother was referred to hospice care.

My grandmother lived about 30 days in hospice. One day in particular she called me in the room and she told me "I just wanted to tell you that you're going to be just fine." It seemed to be a message sent to me through her. It was as if heaven was sending a message to me while simultaneously preparing a home for her. We battled a very similar fight but our outcomes would be completely different.

My grandmother would have been 95 had she lived just two more weeks. It would be easy to say that our age difference alone would warrant us differing outcomes. I submit to you another family member-a cousin diagnosed with breast cancer a few years earlier. She was only a year and a half older than me and passed away just six months before my diagnosis. She and I were so similar. We had similar careers, we both loved to sing but in the arena of breast cancer our outcomes were very different.

I say all of this to pose these questions to you:

Why are you still here?

Why were you allowed to survive?

What is your purpose?

I wonder if you have honestly considered that it is a privilege to be in the land of the living. It is time to figure out your "why" and to put it into action. I suggest you get busy living, and finding out what your purpose is. This will involve identifying your passions or the things that are most important in your life. Your passions act as clues or breadcrumbs that lead you to your purpose or personal destiny. As your purpose and personal destiny begin to be revealed, you will know they are the very reasons why you were created.

I am of the opinion that if you have been afforded more time on this earth, that time is not just for you. 1Peter 4:10 says *"As every man hath received the gift, even so minister the same one to another, as good stewards of the manifold grace of God."* Strongly consider the gifts that God has placed in you. Work hard to bring them to the surface, not only to bless you, but to bless others as well. I am confident God brings us out of situations to take us to something greater. This can be seen so clearly through the children of Israel's exodus and journey in the wilderness. God's plan was not just to bring them out of Egypt but also to take them to their Promised Land, which was Canaan. God's desire is still the same for us today. He brings us out of cancerous conditions to take us to the places He's planned for us-our Promised Land.

I encourage you to finish the unfinished work you have. God is giving you the time and opportunity to get it done.

{9}

WHAT IS YOUR IT?

I went back to work after five months of being off for surgery and chemotherapy. From my view, I had a new lease on life, my spirit was very open, and I felt free. I returned to work with an expanded attitude towards my job. Yet not long after returning to work, I still felt unfulfilled in my work environment.

Discovering My Its

One thing I was clear on — there was nothing more important than living my best life now. I began to ponder what that would look like for me. I purchased a copy of the New York Times bestseller, "The Passion Test" and through a series of questions, I discovered that the top five things most important to me are:

- Inspirational speaking to large groups of women
- Coaching and Motivating others to discover their passions and follow their dreams
- Being healthy and strong and maintaining a regular exercise regiment
- Spending quality time with my family
- Contributing to the care of cancer patients

I was so inspired by what I discovered through the Passion Test, that I became certified to coach others how to discover their passions too!

When I began to put my attention on the things that were most important to me, it became easy to make decisions that better aligned me with my passions. The decision to leave my job was easy. It seemed risky to some in my circle because it was a well branded and stable company. Fear and power of the brand no longer crippled me. My desire to fulfill my passions and to make meaningful contributions in the lives of others far outweighed the perks the job offered.

I now own my own company, Master Your Passions, Inc. through which I facilitate in-person and online workshops helping others to gain clarity on their passions. A Gallup study showed that less than 30% of people are living passionate and fulfilled lives. It is easy to choose in favor of your passions when you are clear on what they are. Now that I am clear on my "its", I hope to be a major catalyst in turning those statistics around.

I left my job on good terms and I have returned once to visit my coworkers whom I had grown to love over the 12 years I worked there. It really saddened me to witness so many of them express their discontent with the working conditions yet for various reasons felt unable to be an agent of change in their current place or somewhere else.

I made a vow not to be "cancer" when it comes to dealing with my coworkers. I do not ever plan to foster behaviors or stir in discontent that will not benefit them or the company.

I also vowed to challenge each of them as opportunity permits. This challenge applies to you in your current condition, be it work or otherwise.

What are you passionate about? What things are most important to you? Who is really to blame if you have not taken the time to answer these questions or have not taken the steps to focus on what you discovered when you did answer them?

I refer to people who continue to exist in toxic and unhealthy working conditions as the "walking dead". Many have dreams, ideas and purpose all buried inside of them, while they tirelessly expect others to affirm and promote them. I identify with this person so well because "it was me." I ask you "is it you?"

I guess the pain of continuing in that condition seems easier to manage than the perceived risks and fears that come with doing something different, something new, something fresh, even something they were purposed and created for. This reminds me of a story I heard once concerning a farmer's whining dog. When questioned why he whined so, the farmer replied that he was lying on a nail. When questioned why the dog would not move to a different spot, the farmer replied, ""Best I can reckon, it doesn't hurt that much."

{10}

WHAT IS HOLDING YOU BACK?

Most of America was still reeling from the economic crisis in 2011, while I was going through my cancer journey. My parents were not exempt and experienced their greatest financial battle I can recall during my lifetime. It was a really stressful time; the lack they were experiencing really took a toll on my mother's spirit. My parents were arguing a lot. My parents and I are like The Three Stooges at times. We do a lot together, including running a small tax practice. Because of the closeness of our relationship and the severity of what they were going through, both of my parents felt comfortable sharing their deepest concerns with me even during my cancer journey.

I recall a day when I had just come home from treatment and was already beginning to feel a little queasy. I found my mother at the kitchen table crying about her inability to afford some much needed medication. This was something she had not experienced before. In that moment, I felt powerless.

I also remember another day that had significant impact on me. I had begun training for the annual breast cancer walk. My mom had been gracious enough to stay with me for a few weeks and assist me in getting my daughter ready for daycare. This allowed me to walk as many as five miles in the early morning before heading to work.

One morning in particular, I woke with a special tugging in my heart to do something extra special for my mom to show her how much I appreciated all that she had done for me. I wrote her a check, and I placed it in the room where she had been sleeping. As I passed my daughter's bedroom, where my mom was assisting her in getting dressed, I said, "Mom, I just wanted to bless you in a special way today." Later she came to my bedroom door with tears in her eyes when she realized how much I had written the check for. She looked so tired and broken as she said, "I've done nothing to warrant this type of money." I can still see the brokenness in her eyes that day and even now I have a hard time holding back the tears that look triggered in me.

Somewhere in the midst of these times, I gained a new determination about my future. From that day forward I decided I would no longer allow someone else to put caps on my income and limit my ability to expand and be all I was called to be. Maybe for me, that was the moment the "nagging of the nail" became intense enough for me to move.

I had first-hand experience in how quickly life and situations can change. I vowed not to let anything stop me from living my best life now. I decided I could no longer be held back.

So what about you, what is holding you back?

Is it the familiarity of where you are? No matter how unfulfilled we find ourselves, there is a tendency to remain in places that are commonplace and what we've grown accustomed to. It is important to realize that holding on to familiar places may be the very thing preventing you from unleashing the greatest potential within you.

Another thing that holds us back is fear. Many people remain in unhealthy relationships because of the fear of what they do not know. As a result, cancerous conditions and toxic situations continue to be the order of each day. There is a false sense of security attached to a check, a hug, or other temporary comfort the relationship may provide. The fear of being alone or having to make it on your own can stifle your ability to move forward into a relationship that will be more meaningful and healthy for you.

In some cases, we are simply afraid to be free. Walking in freedom places more responsibility on you and less blame on others for the good and bad conditions that exist in your life.

Looking back in history when the Emancipation Proclamation was signed and Jim Crow laws were established, many slaves stayed with their masters. They stayed simply because it was what they knew. They had a fear of what they did not know. Many, I am sure, had a mindset and acceptance of captivity. Sometimes we can be conditioned for fear either by our inner agents at work or from outside sources as well.

We have to get clear on our purpose and calling. We must overcome our fears and limiting beliefs. We must understand that failure is sometimes required to move forward.

Conclusion

Cancerous-it was me in both my physical body and in how I operated in relationships and handled disappointments in the workplace. I pray you will examine every facet of your life as you assess "Is it you?" Baseline your findings on the pure definition of cancer as you ask yourself these questions:

1. Do I find myself acting abnormal within the organized groups (i.e. family, work, church, etc.) I am a part of?
2. Do I have a tendency to cause division?
3. Have I been a constant cause for dissension in my family, tension on the job, destruction in other groups I am privileged to be a part of?

I know my usage of parallels between the cancers directly affecting the body and the other cancerous life conditions we face may stir up some controversy. I believe this to be true only in the limited minds of those refusing to see the life threatening effects these destructive patterns cause when we allow them to go untreated in our lives. I am convinced I was predestined to experience every phase of cancer diagnosis and treatment to get clear on just how similar these conditions are.

It is my prayer that none of us will allow where we have been and the negative conditions we have been exposed to determine where we are headed. It is my hope that we will make choices to get healthy and stay healthy in every area of our lives.

With an ever changing world around us, you and I must be willing to early detect conditions that threaten to destroy us at our core. I wish I could promise you a life with constant and flowery beds of ease. I cannot. But I can promise you this: If you will commit all of your ways unto God and trust Him, He will help you to bring forth the deepest desires of your heart. In this posture, you are most equipped to handle the effects of all you face along your journey. I charge you to move forward with a willingness to survive again and again!

DISCUSSION QUESTIONS

These discussion questions are designed for both personal reflection and small-group use and are meant to help you in detecting and treating the things that limit you and seek to destroy you. Please don't focus on providing the "right" answers. What matters most is that you review the bible truths provided and apply what you learn from them to your own life situations. I pray that you will seek God's leading as you work through them.

The scriptures embedded throughout the questions will help keep your focus on God's word. Feel free to use the space provided to write your answers. Consider using a pencil for ease of altering your responses as you gain clarity. May He bless, keep, restore and revive you during this time that you spend in His word!

CHAPTER 1: THE TRUTH ABOUT CANCER

1. Think of a discomforting situation you have now or have had recently. Ask yourself what positive story or thought can I give to this situation. How does Philippians 4:8 teach us to consider things?

2. Looking back to what you've identified in question #1, can you now see a greater purpose than what you understood in the midst of the situation? What assurances do we get in Romans 8:28?

3. Reflect back to the prayer of strength highlighted on pages 19-20. Consider this prayer as a daily meditation.

4. Can you think of a time when you were able to strengthen and encourage someone else? How did that make you feel? According to Hebrews 3:13 how often should we seek to encourage others?

5. Consider the areas of your life you may be mistaking denial for faith. How can John 14:26 aid you in knowing the difference?

CHAPTER 2: DO YOU HAVE IT?

1. With a better understanding that our normal God-given desires and emotions become abnormal, what areas of your life may presently be operating in abnormal or cancerous and destructive ways?

2. Evaluate your busyness with church activities matched against your quiet time and personal relationship with God. Do they complement or contrast each other? How can the lessons of two sisters Mary and Martha in Luke 10:38-42 help you to understand the importance of balance in this area?

3. Have you ever found yourself longing for something you were confident God had delivered you from (i.e. relationship, work situation, food or drug addition, excessive shopping behavior, etc.)? What encouragement can you receive from Paul in Philippians 3:12-14?

4. How important to you are your mate's and friends' relationships with God? How do you feel those relationships impact your relationship with each other? Do you feel 2 Corinthians 6:14-18 applies to all relationships and friendships? Why or why not?

5. According to Ephesians 4:31, what amount of bitterness is appropriate to hold onto? How does this passage admonish us to respond even in times of frustration? (Ephesians 4:29-31)

CHAPTER 3: WHAT IS YOUR TREATMENT PLAN?

1. When have you experienced a personal revival? If it has been awhile, consider these verses as you seek personal revival today: Isaiah 59:1-3, James 4:8, Psalm 19:12, 2 Timothy 2:21

2. Can you identify any hardships or challenges you have faced that resulted in you growing closer to God? How do 1 Peter 5:10 and James 1:2-4 help us to respond when facing challenges?

3. Consider using the scriptures on page 41 as a part of your daily affirmations.

4. Reflecting back to your response in Chapter 3, Question #1, have you determined the root cause of the condition? If you were unable to identify any present conditions, have you gotten clear on the root causes of prior conditions so that you can focus there in an effort not to experience a recurrence?

5. In plant life, the root is that portion of the plant which nourishes the whole. Read Colossians 3:5-8 and Romans 8:13. Why is it important to get to the "root" causes of our conditions?

CHAPTER 4: WHO IS YOUR SUPPORT SYSTEM?

1. Do you feel you have adequate support for this current season in your life? If not, identify the reservations you have for asking for additional help. Pray about your reservations using Matthew 7:7-8 to unlock any limiting beliefs about what's available to you.

2. How have you limited your opportunity to receive help/support in the past?

3. Are there areas of your life that you have preferred to operate or handle in isolation? Evaluate how operating in this manner has served you. How might Ecclesiastes 4:12 help you to see the importance of joining together with other believers to overcome life's challenges?

4. Determine one action step you can take today or in the near future to "pay it forward" to someone who has supported you in some way.

CHAPTER 5: SIDE EFFECTS

1. What do you think are the spiritual side effects of a healthy spiritual life?

2. What side effects have you experienced as a result of the conditions you identified in Chapter 3, Question #1?

3. What does Galatians 5:22-23 tell us are characteristics of the fruit of the spirit? Consider how these are evident in your life when you are properly rooted in the word of God.

4. What losses, if any, can you identify in your life that were beneficial for the transformation you now have?

CHAPTER 6: HOW DO YOU LIVE IN SURVIVORVILLE?

1. On a scale of 1 to 10 with 10 being the most successful state of thriving, rate whether you are merely existing or thriving.

2. What is one thing you have survived or overcome?

3. Are you open to sharing your story with others where appropriate? If not, why?

4. How do you view yourself on this side of the situation you identified in Question #2? If the same, consider if it is because you were thriving prior to the situation. If different, consider if it is because you were not.

CHAPTER 7: WHOSE REPORT WILL YOU BELIEVE?

1. How have you allowed doubt to operate in your life?

2. Now that you notice, do you recognize certain areas that you consistently tend to doubt most?

3. Read Mark 9:23. Consider adding it to your daily affirmation list.

4. Real Mark 11:22-24. In the areas noted in Question #1, begin to pray this scripture and affirm these words concerning the areas where doubt has been influencing you most.

5. Have you ever journaled? Begin a routine of journaling to capture your thoughts and prayers and to be able to reflect on changes in your beliefs as you move forward.

CHAPTER 8: WHY ARE YOU HERE?

1. Have you given consideration to God's calling on your life? What does Thessalonians 5:16-18 tell us we should be constantly doing?

2. Review your response to Chapter 1, Question #2. Pray for the confidence that all of your situations are working for your good.

3. Read Jeremiah 29:11. Do you trust these words at all times? Be honest in your assessment. If not, why?

4. How does Deuteronomy 31:6 instruct us to walk in the face of adversity and hardships?

5. What does John 15:8 suggest we should be doing in this life? What evidence is there that you are bearing fruit? If you cannot identify any, why not?

6. What is one action step you can take today or in the near future to begin a fruit-filled life?

CHAPTER 9: WHAT IS YOUR IT?

1. What are the top five things that are most important to you?

2. How much focus have you given to these areas?

3. Read Ecclesiastes 11 to gain a better understanding on the importance of investing in yourself and in your life.

4. What limitation have you placed on your ability to have what you've identified in Question #1?

CHAPTER 10: WHAT IS HOLDING YOU BACK?

1. What, if anything, is holding you back from living the life you dream of?

2. Read Philippians 3:12-14 again. What does this scripture imply about the future in comparison to the past?

3. Pray for increased faith to let go of the areas relating to your past that hinder you from moving forward.

4. Where does fear come from? If you are uncertain, read 2 Timothy 1:7. Where can you now be confident fear does not come from?

5. Read Hebrews 11:1. Are the familiar things we see and have grown accustomed to a part of our faith? What benefit can these things serve? What limitations can they cause?

6. When time permits, read Hebrews 11 in its entirety as you seek to unleash the fears and familiar things that are holding you from your greater purpose.

AFTERWORD

It's truly amazing how God works in us when we are open. Upon the completion of this book, I received a word one morning-a sort of urging to spend some time talking about prayer. To be quite honest, I felt a sort of conviction about not having ensured my readers know beyond a shadow of a doubt the importance and impact of prayer in their lives, especially in overcoming cancerous conditions of all kinds and cutting off cancerous cells or carriers at their root. As I reflected on this issue, this passage of scripture came to mind:

14 And when they were come to the multitude, there came to him a certain man, kneeling down to him, and saying, 15 Lord, have mercy on my son: for he is lunatick, and sore vexed: for ofttimes he falleth into the fire, and oft into the water. 16 And I brought him to thy disciples, and they could not cure him. 17 Then Jesus answered and said, O faithless and perverse generation, how long shall I be with you? how long shall I suffer you? bring him hither to me. 18 And Jesus rebuked the devil; and he departed out of him: and the child was cured from that very hour. 19 Then came the disciples to Jesus apart, and said, Why could not we cast him out? 20 And Jesus said unto them, Because of your unbelief: for verily I say unto you, If ye have faith as a grain of mustard seed, ye shall say unto this mountain, Remove hence to yonder place; and it shall remove; and nothing shall be impossible unto you. 21 Howbeit this kind goeth not out but by prayer and fasting. (Matthew 17:14-21)

The conditions discussed in this book, "Cancer-Us", are not surface level conditions and often cannot be easily disbanded. Much like the conditions of the son highlighted in the passage of scripture, these things can only be removed through prayer and fasting.

Prayer is communication with God. Effective communication with anyone involves both speaking and listening at the appropriate times. The same is true in our communication with God.

Fasting, as it is used in the passage, involves abstaining from food while focusing on prayer. This can mean refraining from snacks between meals, skipping one or two meals a day, abstaining only from certain foods, or a total fast from all foods for an entire day or longer. I am of the opinion that a person can fast from anything. The key of the spiritual fast is a denial of self and focus on God.

Prayer and fasting work in concert together. Speak to God about things to give up as you seek Him in a more intimate, personal and powerful way. Listen for Him to direct you either through His word, someone else, or simply placing clarity of thought about an issue in your mind. Pray for self-control and discipline to stay the course and remain faithful, remembering that the conditions you most want to rid yourself of may be totally dependent on your ability to do so.

ABOUT THE AUTHOR

Dywuana Morris Sykes is an inspirational speaker, author, entrepreneur and coach. As a highly acclaimed national speaker in the U.S., Dywuana Sykes has delivered inspiring messages to a variety of groups, ranging from large church congregations to Fortune 100 Companies. Her dynamic delivery and recharging inspiration as well as her width of business experience have earned raves from audiences as intimate as 25 and as vast as 2500.

Dywuana is a graduate of the University of Memphis and Middle Tennessee State University. Dywuana is also a licensed Certified Public Accountant. For the past twelve years, she has maintained a part-time tax practice, Integrity Tax and Bookkeeping.

Dywuana currently serves as Chaplain for the Desoto County (MS) Alumnae Chapter of Delta Sigma Theta Sorority, Inc. She holds ministry positions of small group leader and mentor facilitating the spiritual growth of women in her church.

Dywuana is founder and CEO of Master Your Passions, Inc. Through her organization, Dywuana assists clients in connecting with their passions and learning new ways of handling challenging situations. She accomplishes this via workshops, personal coaching, group coaching and teleseminars.

Her ultimate passion is being an inspirational speaker to men and women across this nation. Through her messages, she gives them hope and inspiration to forge ahead even in the midst of adversity.

Dywuana currently resides in Olive Branch, Mississippi. She is married to Kenneth Sykes and they are blessed to have one daughter, Kendall Elyse. Visit www.dywuanasykes.com.

NOTES

NOTES

Made in the USA
San Bernardino, CA
23 September 2014